CHECKERBOARD BIOGRAPHY LIBRARY

EXPLORERS

Henry
Hudson

Kristin Petrie

ABDO
Publishing Company

visit us at
www.abdopublishing.com

Published by ABDO Publishing Company, 4940 Viking Drive, Edina, Minnesota 55435.
Copyright © 2007 by Abdo Consulting Group, Inc. International copyrights reserved in all
countries. No part of this book may be reproduced in any form without written permission from
the publisher. The Checkerboard Library™ is a trademark and logo of ABDO Publishing
Company.

Printed in the United States.

Cover Photos: Corbis, North Wind
Interior Photos: Corbis pp. 5, 7, 13, 15, 19, 21; Getty Images pp. 11, 27; North Wind pp. 9, 10, 17,
    23, 29

Series Coordinator: Heidi M. Dahmes
Editors: Rochelle Baltzer, Heidi M. Dahmes
Art Direction & Cover Design: Neil Klinepier
Interior Design & Maps: Dave Bullen

Library of Congress Cataloging-in-Publication Data

Petrie, Kristin, 1970-
  Henry Hudson / Kristin Petrie.
    p. cm. -- (Explorers)
  Includes bibliographical references (p.) and index.
  ISBN-10 1-59679-741-X
  ISBN-13 978-1-59679-741-3
  1. Hudson, Henry, d. 1611--Juvenile literature. 2. America--Discovery and exploration--
English--Juvenile literature. 3. Explorers--America--Biography--Juvenile literature. 4.
Explorers--Great Britain--Biography--Juvenile literature. I. Title II. Series: Petrie, Kristin,
1970- . Explorers.

E129.H8P48 2006
910'.92--dc22
                                                                        2005017127

Contents

Henry Hudson

Henry Hudson was a brave and determined explorer. Not frozen fingers, seasickness, or even icebergs could keep this Englishman from fulfilling his life's mission. Between 1607 and 1611, Hudson made four voyages into the freezing waters of the north seas. His goal was to find a shorter route from Europe to Asia through the Arctic Ocean.

Hudson was not alone. Many European countries sent explorers in search of a new route to Asia. European lifestyles depended on trade with Asian countries. Europeans desired luxurious silks from Asia. And, they used Asian spices to season their food and to keep it fresh.

However, land routes to Asia were long and unreliable. Religious and territorial wars could stop trading in an instant. Plus, Spain and Portugal controlled the known sea routes to Asia. Other European countries were desperate for another way to continue trading. So they looked to the north.

1271
Polo left for Asia

1295
Polo returned to Italy

1254
Marco Polo born

1275
Polo met Kublai Khan

Today, Henry Hudson's accomplishments are remembered by the river *(above)*, strait, and bay that are named in his honor.

Hudson is one of the most well-known explorers to search for a shorter route to Asia. He searched north of Europe for a water passage. Later, he continued his search in the northern waters of North America. Hudson's discoveries there led other explorers to this area in an attempt to find a northwest passage.

1460 or 1474
Juan Ponce de León born

1480
Ferdinand Magellan born

1324
Polo died

1475
Vasco Núñez de Balboa born

Early Life

Very little is known about Henry Hudson's early life. Even his birth date is a mystery. But, scholars believe he was born around 1565. The Hudson family lived in or near the busy port city of London, England.

Henry's grandfather helped form the **Muscovy Company**. The company ran trade voyages to Russia. There, the English exchanged goods for **tallow**, hemp, **cordage**, and other products. The Muscovy Company was the **sponsor** of the exploratory voyages. It hoped to find a new trading route to Asia.

Henry's father was a wealthy man. He and his wife had eight sons. All of the Hudson boys worked at sea as captains or traders.

1500
Balboa joined expedition to South America

1493
Ponce de León joined expedition to New World

1502
Ponce de León became governor of Higüey

Would You?

Would you enjoy living in a port city? Do you think it would inspire you to become a sailor or maybe even an explorer? What lands would you like to explore?

London was the largest and busiest port in the world until World War II.

1508
Ponce de León's first expedition

1514
Ponce de León knighted by King Ferdinand II

1513
Ponce de León's second expedition, discovered Florida and the Gulf Stream; Balboa was the first European to sight the Pacific Ocean

Early Work

Like most men of his time, Henry's life and work revolved around the sea. As a young man, Henry worked on ships. He likely started as a cabin boy and worked his way up. He learned how to cook, handle sails, read the weather, and care for a ship. As captain later in his career, he kept a ship log. So, he must also have learned to read and write.

Some historians believe that in 1587, Henry sailed with an English explorer named John Davis. Davis crossed the Atlantic Ocean and combed the Canadian Arctic for a passage to Asia.

On this voyage, Davis noted a large channel of water near the Labrador Sea. He named it the Furious Overfall because of its raging waters. Today, this is known as Hudson Strait.

Davis led the way for explorers who were interested in this region. His voyages may have sparked Henry's determination to search for a northwest passage.

1520
Magellan discovered the Strait of Magellan

1554
Walter Raleigh born

1519
Magellan led expedition to Spice Islands; Balboa died

1521
Ponce de León's third expedition, died in Cuba; Magellan died

Would You?

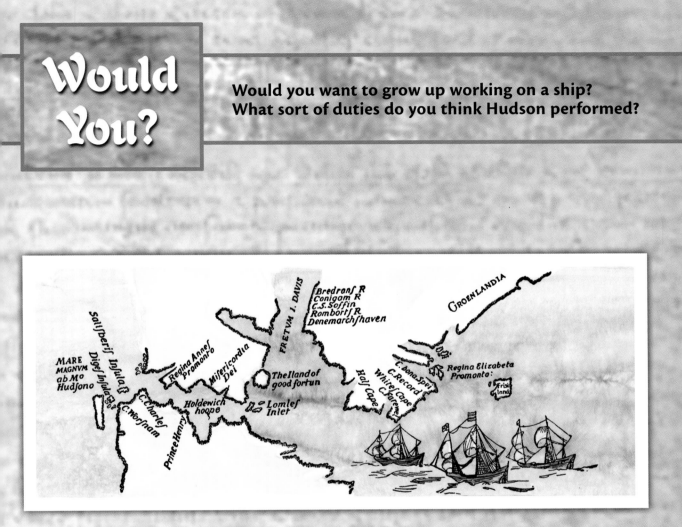

**Using what he had been taught as a young man,
Henry later drew this map of his voyages.**

Family

Henry's name does not appear in written records until 1607. Still, it is known that Henry married a woman named Katherine. She was strong willed and determined, much like her husband.

Katherine and Henry had three sons named Richard, John, and Oliver. John sailed with his father on each of Henry's four historic voyages.

Richard lived a very different life from John and his father. Richard worked as a trader for the **Dutch East India Company**. So, he lived and worked in Japan and India.

The Dutch East India Company was founded in 1602.

Little is recorded about Henry's son Oliver. But, some historians believe that he wrote the journal of his father's 1587 voyage, which was published in 1612.

1580
John Smith born

1585
Raleigh knighted by Queen Elizabeth I

1565
Henry Hudson born

1584–1589
Raleigh sponsored expeditions

The portraits of Henry that exist today were probably painted after his death. These were created solely from descriptions. So, they may not even show how he really looked!

First Voyage

In Hudson's time, scholars believed that the sun shone continuously for five months at the North Pole. They hoped the sun's heat would melt the ice so ships could sail through the Arctic waters. The scholars thought that traveling through the North Pole would be the fastest route to Asia yet!

Hudson's experience at sea had made him skilled at navigation and map reading. So, the **Muscovy Company** hired Hudson. The company instructed him to find a northeast passage to Asia through the North Pole.

For the voyage, Hudson received a small ship called the *Hopewell*. He selected a crew of ten men, plus his son John. The group set sail from Gravesend, England, in April 1607.

After six weeks, Hudson spotted Greenland. The crew sailed north along the frozen land, charting its eastern coastline. When icy waters made it impossible to continue, Hudson turned to the east.

1595
Raleigh led first expedition

1588
Raleigh helped defeat the Spanish Armada

1606
Smith joined expedition to North America

The *Hopewell* reached Spitsbergen, near Norway. Spitsbergen is an island just 700 miles (1,130 km) from the North Pole. No explorer had sailed so far north! Unfortunately, walls of ice forced Hudson to turn back toward England. Hudson concluded that it was impossible to sail through the North Pole.

Hudson proved that the North Pole stays frozen even in the summer.

Discoveries

Hudson's first attempt to find a northeast passage to Asia had failed. However, he and his crew had made many other discoveries. Near Spitsbergen, Hudson recorded the sight of strange birds waddling on the ice. These animals had black backs and white bellies. Hudson had spotted the now-extinct great auk!

Hudson's crew also noted many seals and walrus. And on shore they discovered deer antlers, whale bones, and flocks of barnacle geese.

In the water, the *Hopewell* encountered whales. At times, there were so many that they brushed the side of the ship. One whale even got caught on a fishing line!

These findings led to the start of the English **whaling** industry near Spitsbergen. Soon, ships from England began harvesting the whales. The Dutch followed shortly after.

1607
Hudson's first expedition

1609
Hudson's third expedition

1608
Hudson's second expedition

Walrus tusks would soon be desired by traders.

The **whaling** industry grew quickly. The Dutch and the English used whale **blubber** for oil and **baleen** for garments and tools. Within ten years of Hudson's voyage, the waters of Spitsbergen were nearly empty of whales.

1614
Smith led expedition to North America, charted and named New England

1610-1611
Hudson's last expedition, he died

1616
Raleigh's second expedition

Second Voyage

One year after Hudson's first departure, the **Muscovy Company sponsored** his next voyage. Hudson was to again search for a northeast passage to Asia. This time, he planned to sail along Russia's northern coast. This was one of the most hostile places on Earth!

On April 22, 1608, the *Hopewell* left London with Hudson and his crew of 15 men. The voyage was rocky from the start. The ice and the cold made the voyagers miserable.

By the end of May, the *Hopewell* passed the northern tip of Norway. It headed for the islands of Novaya Zemlya off Russia's coast. Hudson searched the coastlines for a passage. Not surprisingly, ice blocks forced him to turn south.

In July, the waters were so icy that Hudson gave up his search. But instead of returning to England, Hudson secretly turned the *Hopewell* toward North America.

After several weeks, the crew figured out that Hudson was seeking a northwest passage. They angrily refused to

1618
Raleigh died

1637
Jacques Marquette born

1645
Louis Jolliet born

1631
Smith died

1643
René-Robert Cavelier de La Salle born

obey his orders. With the entire crew against him, Hudson had to turn back. The *Hopewell* arrived in Gravesend on August 26. The **Muscovy Company** was unhappy with the unsuccessful voyage.

The *Hopewell* had to hold up to more ice in the frozen waters of northern Russia. So, it was strengthened with extra planks.

Third Voyage

Although discouraged, Hudson did not stop his work for long. Rejected by the English, Hudson now turned to the Dutch. They were also interested in a new route to Asia. Soon, the **Dutch East India Company** requested Hudson's services. So, Hudson moved his family to Amsterdam, Netherlands. He began sailing for the Dutch.

Hudson agreed to return to Novaya Zemlya and continue the search for a northeast passage. The trading company insisted that this was the only area he could explore. It knew of Hudson's interest in seeking a northwest passage.

Hudson faced problems before he even left port. He selected a mixture of 20 English and Dutch sailors for his crew. Many of the sailors did not speak the others' language. Hudson himself did not speak Dutch! In addition, the ship he received was small and lightweight. The *Half Moon* was not made for rough, icy waters.

1669
La Salle explored Ohio region

1666
La Salle sailed to Canada

1673
Marquette and Jolliet explored the Mississippi River

The *Half Moon* set sail from Amsterdam, Netherlands.

These difficulties didn't stop Hudson. On April 6, 1609, the *Half Moon* set sail. Unfortunately, more problems arose. The Dutch sailors were not used to the cold, choppy waters north of Europe. The crew neared **mutiny**. But, Hudson calmed the men by making a deal.

Hudson convinced his crew to sail west to the warmer waters of North America. Ignoring the work contract, Hudson and his crew crossed the Atlantic Ocean. They encountered many storms along the way.

In July, the *Half Moon* reached the coast of present-day Canada. Later that month, the crew set foot on the coast of today's Maine. There, they met and traded peacefully with natives. However, the Europeans soon became greedy. They stole everything they could from the natives before sailing south.

Hudson did not scold his crew. He cared only about finding a northwest passage. Hudson searched up and down the East Coast. He sailed as far south as Chesapeake Bay. Following this, he turned back to the north.   He briefly explored Delaware Bay.

1675
Marquette died

1682
La Salle's second Mississippi River expedition

1679
La Salle's first Mississippi River expedition

The natives offered Hudson and his crew beaver skins and other furs for trade.

In September, Hudson reached a large bay at the site of today's New York City, New York. He sailed north up the present-day Hudson River and claimed the area for the Dutch.

The *Half Moon* sailed for days up the great waterway. Reaching shallow waters, Hudson realized the river did not lead to the Pacific Ocean. Near present-day Albany, New York, Hudson turned the ship back toward the Atlantic and home.

1687
La Salle died

1684
La Salle's third Mississippi River expedition

1700
Jolliet died

Return

The *Half Moon* reached Dartmouth, England, on November 7, 1609. No one knows why Hudson sailed to England rather than to the Netherlands. He had disobeyed his Dutch **sponsors** by sailing to North America. So, perhaps he feared their reactions.

As it turned out, King James I of England wasn't pleased with Hudson either. Hudson's discoveries had benefited another country. So, Hudson was arrested for treason. He was told he could sail for no other country but England.

The Dutch crew members sailed the *Half Moon* back to the Netherlands. Hudson's voyage logs were on board. Hudson and the other English crew members never returned to the Netherlands.

Meanwhile, wealthy English merchants heard of Hudson's discoveries in North America and were excited! Good trading, large natural ports, and fertile countryside were profitable discoveries.

1770
William Clark born

1786
Sacagawea born

1774
Meriwether Lewis born

1800
Sacagawea captured

James I was king of
England from 1603 to 1625.

Soon, the **British East India Company**, the **Muscovy Company**, and several private **sponsors** contributed to Hudson's fourth voyage. The backers provided a large ship called the *Discovery*. Hudson selected 22 men for the expedition.

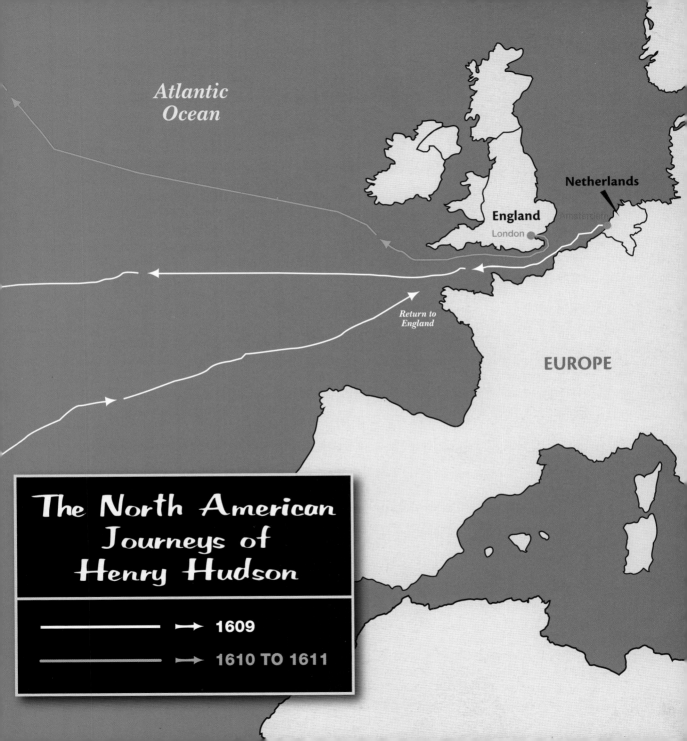

Atlantic
Ocean

Netherlands

England
London

Amsterdam

Return to England

EUROPE

The North American Journeys of Henry Hudson

⟶	**1609**
⟶	**1610 TO 1611**

Final Voyage

On April 17, 1610, the *Discovery* left London. Hudson hoped to reach Asia from the waters north of North America. Only 8 of the 23 men on board would ever see England again.

In June, the *Discovery* reached the northern Canadian coast and continued sailing west. On June 25, Hudson directed his ship into a familiar channel of water. This was the strait Davis had named the Furious Overfall.

The *Discovery* sailed about 500 miles (800 km) down the waterway. It widened into a large body of water that we now know as Hudson Bay. However, Hudson thought they had found the passage to the Pacific Ocean. The crew sailed south while dreaming of the warmer waters of Asia.

At the south end of Hudson Bay, the crew hit a dead end. By this time, the weather was even colder and the waters were icy. The crew sailed aimlessly. Then, they spent a

1804
Lewis and Clark began exploring the Pacific Northwest

1806
Lewis and Clark returned to Missouri

1805
Sacagawea joined the Lewis and Clark expedition

Would You?

Would you sign up for an expedition to Arctic regions? Do you think Hudson's men knew what kind of weather to expect? What type of clothing do you think they wore?

Hudson and his crew probably suffered through temperatures as cold as -49 degrees Fahrenheit (-45°C).

terrible winter on land. After the first few months, they found nothing to eat but moss and frogs. Not only were they bitterly cold, but they also suffered from **scurvy**.

Deserted

By June 12, 1611, the water had thawed enough for the *Discovery* to sail again. Hudson announced that the search would continue. However, the crew was worried they would not survive. They only had enough food to last two weeks.

Some crew members planned a **mutiny**. On June 22, they forced Hudson, his son John, and seven other crew members into a small boat. Then, they sailed the *Discovery* home without them. No one knows what happened to Hudson and the abandoned men.

Without their captain, the mutineers had a rough voyage home. Back in England, they were tried for mutiny. But, they were found innocent. Their stories about Hudson Strait and Hudson Bay reinforced the hope of finding a northwest passage to Asia.

Henry Hudson searched persistently for a passage to Asia. In the process, he sailed farther north than any explorer before him. And, he navigated the entire Hudson Strait.

1812
Sacagawea died

1856
Robert Edwin Peary born

1809
Lewis died

1838
Clark died

1881
Peary entered the U.S. Navy

Hudson and eight men were left to fend for themselves in the cold waters of the Hudson Bay.

Hudson's discoveries provided valuable information for future explorations. And, his brave efforts led to Dutch and English colonization of North America.

1893
Peary's first expedition

1909
Peary's third expedition, reached the North Pole

1905
Peary's second expedition

1920
Peary died

Glossary

baleen - of or relating to the tough, hornlike material that hangs from the upper jaw of certain whales. Whales use baleen to filter food.

blubber - a layer of fat in whales and other marine mammals. Blubber provides the whale with insulation, food storage, and padding.

British East India Company - a company that opened India and the Far East to trade.

cordage - ropes or cords made by twisting plant fibers.

Dutch East India Company - a company formed to expand Dutch trade and maintain close contact between the Dutch government and its colonies.

Muscovy Company - a group of English merchants that traded with Russia.

mutiny - open rebellion against lawful authority, especially by sailors or soldiers against their officers.

scurvy - a fatal disease caused by a lack of vitamin C.

sponsor - a person or a group of people who support someone, often financially.

tallow - the melted fat of cattle and sheep used in making candles and soaps.

whaling - the act, business, or work of hunting and killing whales for their oil, flesh, and bone.

Saying It

baleen - buh-LEEN
Gravesend - GRAYVZ-EHND
Muscovy - MUHS-koh-vee
Novaya Zemlya - noh-vuh-yuh zehm-lee-AH
Spitsbergen - SPIHTS-buhr-guhn

Web Sites

To learn more about Henry Hudson, visit ABDO Publishing Company on the World Wide Web at **www.abdopublishing.com**. Web sites about Hudson are featured on our Book Links page. These links are routinely monitored and updated to provide the most current information available.

Index

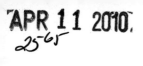